CW00590035

Porsche
Boxster and Boxster S
(1996 to 2005)

Peter Morgan
PMM Books

First published 2004
Second Edition 2005

ISBN 0 9549990 0 2

PMM Books, an imprint of Peter Morgan Media Ltd.
PO Box 2561, Marlborough, Wiltshire, SN8 1YD, Great Britain.
Telephone: +44 1672 514038
E-mail: sales@pmmbooks.com
Website: www.pmmbooks.com

Ultimate Buyers' Guide
Porsche Boxster and Boxster S
1996 to 2005
Contents

Porsche Boxster and Boxster S
1996 to 2005

Introduction

This Ultimate Buyers' Guide helps you identify and buy the Porsche Boxster and Boxster S, manufactured between 1996 and still in production in 2005.

The guide includes facts and figures, year by year changes, special models and information on colours and the generally-available options available for all the models.

The buying section tells you what to look for when viewing a Boxster and gives invaluable tips on how to select the most desirable models.

From its introduction in 1996, the Boxster has proven to be an enduring success in the marketplace. In more than eight years of production, during which over 160,000 cars were delivered, the popular roadster has remained unequalled by its competition. As importantly, it has played a pivotal role in the Porsche's business success over the past decade, helping to haul the company back to profitability after years of too much dependency on the iconic 911 models.

The development has been continuous. In 1999, the engine capacity was extended from 2.5-litres to 2.7-litres, while the addition of the 3.2-litre Boxster S extended the model's market superiority. Another major upgrade followed in 2003.

The 2005 Boxsters mark yet another fresh chapter in the Boxster's development. And so confident were Porsche of the winning formula that a brand new coupe version was announced in early 2005.

The Boxster's success in the used marketplace was almost inevitable. In almost every year of its production, new car buyers had to wait months for their cars and this shortage of supply has kept used prices high. The Boxster's desirability is as much to do with its sharp performance as its verstaility and ageless styling. Generally, the Boxster has a good reputation for reliability and longevity.

Maintenance costs have also proven to be on the same level as a typical prestige mid-size car, with both the official networks and independent specialists meeting owners' needs.

For impartial advice on suitable service centres for your Boxster, the best places to buy spare parts and other useful contacts, I would advise you join your national Porsche club.

This guide aims to give you all the technical information you need to select and buy a Boxster. If you are unfamiliar with the risks of buying a used model, then for increased peace of mind, have any potential purchase properly inspected by a Porsche-only specialist.

Peter Morgan,
Marlborough,
Great Britain

Timeline for the Boxster and Boxster S

This timeline (and the references used throughout the text) often refers to the automobile industry's model years. For instance, a 1999 model would be defined as being produced between 1st August 1998 and 31st July 1999.

January 1993
Boxster concept car revealed at Detroit Motor Show.

March 1996
Boxster (Type 986) with 204bhp (150kW) 2.5-litre, water-cooled flat-6 cylinder engine announced. 5-speed gearbox or 5-speed Tiptronic automatic. LHD production starts October 1996. US and UK deliveries start early 1997.

October 1998
Boxster assembly begins at the Valmet factory in Uuisikaupunki, Finland. Chassis numbers have 'U' instead of 'S' as 11th digit.

August 1999
Uprated 220bhp (162kW) 2.7-litre engine for Boxster. E-gas electronic throttle. Alcantara fabric interior. New Boxster S with 252bhp (185kW) 3.2-litre engine, 6-speed gearbox. Part leather interior standard, double skin roof and POSIP side airbag protection introduced. Tiptronic upgraded with 'instantaneous' function.

August 2002
Boxster maximum power increased to 228bhp (168kW), with Boxster S rising to 260bhp (191kW). Glass rear window, new front bumper, new spoiler, grey turn signal lenses. S gets uprated gearbox, new wheels.

September 2003
'50 years of the 550 Spyder' anniversary Boxster S with 266bhp (196kW) engine and GT-silver paint.

September 2004
80 per cent new (Type 987) Boxster and Boxster S announced. Boxster with 240bhp (176kW) and Boxster S 280bhp (206kW). Upgraded PSM with optional active suspension.

Boxster S in Speed Yellow

Facts, figures and performance
Boxster and Boxster S

Bodyshell
Galvanised steel unitary construction, 2-seat roadster bodyshell with 2 doors and mid-mounted engine. Luggage compartments front and rear. Hot dip zinc coating with 10 year warranty against rust perforation. Driver and passenger airbags standard. Porsche Side Impact Protection System (POSIP) side airbag system fitted from 2000 models. Electrically-operated convertible roof.

Plastic fuel tank mounted behind front compartment: capacity: 64 litres (inc. 10 litre reserve. 14.08 imp. gallons; 16.90 US gallons)

Engine
Type M96, all-aluminium, water-cooled flat-six cylinder engine with dry sump lubrication system.

Four valves per cylinder operated by four chain-driven, overhead camshafts (2 per bank), with Porsche Variocam variable valve timing and hydraulic valve play adjustment. Bosch Motronic M5.2 engine management for ignition and sequential fuel injection, with Lambda control. Anti-knock sensing.

Capacity: 2.5: 2480cc; 2.7: 2687cc; S: 3179cc

Maximum power: 2.5: 204bhp (150kW) at 6000rpm. 2.7: 220bhp (162kW) at 6400rpm. 2003: 228bhp (168kW) at 6300rpm. S: 252bhp (185kW) at 6250rpm; 2003: 260bhp at 6200rpm. S '550': 266bhp at 6,200rpm.

Maximum torque: 2.5: 245Nm (181 lb.ft) at 4500rpm. 2.7: 260Nm (192lb.ft) at 4750rpm. 2003: 260Nm (192 lb.ft) at 4700rpm. S: 305Nm (225 lb.ft) at 4500rpm; 2003: 310Nm at 4700rpm; S '550': 310Nm (229lb.ft) at 4,600rpm

Transmission
Boxster: 5-speed, Boxster S: 6-speed manual gearbox. Hydraulic clutch operation and optional limited slip differential.

Optional Tiptronic S 5-speed automatic transmission with manual and Tip-shift modes.

Suspension and steering
Front: Independent MacPherson design with coil spring over telescopic shock absorber, lower control arm and anti-roll bar.

Rear: Coil spring over telescopic shock absorber with multi-link independent design. Anti-roll bar.

Power-assisted rack and pinion steering.

Brakes, wheels and tyres
Twin-circuit system with brake servo, with Antilock Braking System (ABS) and optional traction control.

Ventilated disc brakes with 4-piston calipers all round. 5-spoke cast aluminium alloy wheels all round in sizes and designs dependent on model, option specification and year of manufacture.

At introduction: 6J x 16 with 205/55 tyres front and 7J x 16 with 225/50 tyres rear. Optional 17-inch wheels with 205/50 tyres front and 255/40 tyres rear or 18-inch wheels with 225/40 tyres front and 265/35 tyres rear.

Performance

Acceleration 0 to 62mph (seconds): 2.5: 6.9; 2.7: 6.6; 2003: 6.4. S: 5.9; 2003: 5.7

(Tiptronic S: 2.5: 7.6 seconds; 2.7: 7.4 seconds; 2003: 7.3. S: 6.5 seconds; 2003: 6.4)

Maximum speed: 2.5: 149mph; 2.7: 155mph; 2003: 157mph. S: 162mph; 2003: 164mph

(Tiptronic S: 2.5: 146mph; 2.7: 152mph; 2003: 154mph. S: 158mph: 2003: 160mph)

Typical fuel consumption (mixed cycle): 2.5: 29 to 33mpg; 2.7: 26 to 30mpg; S: 25 to 27mpg

Will it fit?

Length: 4315mm (170 inches)
Width: 1780mm (70.1 inches)
Height: 1290mm (50.8 inches)
Turning circle: 10.90 metres (35.8 feet)
Kerb weight: 2.5: 1250kg; 2.7: 1260-1275kg; S: 1295-1320kg.

For Tiptronic S versions add 50kg

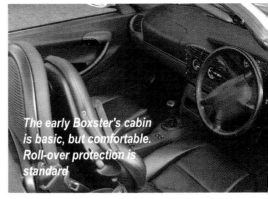

The early Boxster's cabin is basic, but comfortable. Roll-over protection is standard

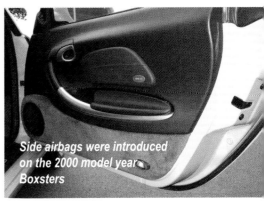

Side airbags were introduced on the 2000 model year Boxsters

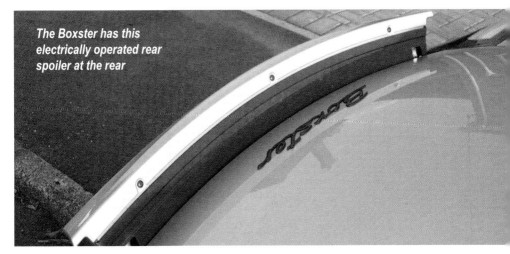

The Boxster has this electrically operated rear spoiler at the rear

Porsche Boxster

Porsche Boxster background

When the Boxster design concept was unveiled at the Detroit Auto Show in January 1993, it caused a sensation. At the time, the world was coming out of a severe economic recession and Porsche, like every other car manufacturer ,was experiencing hard times. Nevertheless, the Boxster would prove to be the company's saviour.

In 1992, the decision had been made to embark on a brand new common platform product development that would yield not one, but two brand new models by the mid to late 1990s. The first would be a complete makeover of the ageing 911 design, which included a brand new, water-cooled six cylinder engine. The second was a radical departure – a two-seat roadster aimed at the lucrative mid-priced sports car segment.

This segment had been a happy hunting ground for Porsche in earlier years. The market potential had been proven first by the 1970s 924 and later, the 944. Despite complaints by 911 fans that the cheaper models were reducing the exclusivity of the marque, Porsche knew that their survival couldn't be allowed to depend on just one model. The cheaper Porsche was an essential step in a strategy aimed at broadening the product range. But there were risks.

1993 Boxster concept car recalled the 550 Spyder racing car of the 1950s

Both the 924 and the 944 had sold strongly in times of strong economic growth and then sales had dived when the markets had turned. Unlike the 911 (that sold to more wealthy individuals less affected by economic ups and downs), the 'entry level' Porsches were exposed to the fickleness of the world's economies.

But in 1992-93, when the company's back was to the wall, the importance of introducing new models couldn't be underestimated. So while the 968 propped up Porsche's presence in the mid-price segment during this time, the Boxster's design gathered momentum.

The philosophy combined the best of modern mid-engined sports car design with a healthy dose of Porsche nostalgia. Much was made of the show car's lines, that recalled the first proper Porsche racing car in the 1950s, the 550 Spyder. While the shape couldn't be described as fully retro, skillfully-added design cues to the 550 included the upswept rear wings, the side air scoops and the rounded rear end.

But while the new car recalled the halcyon days of the past, this was a concept that pointed strongly to the future. The deformable plastic front and rear bumpers, combined with the raked windscreen, gave the car a purposeful – and modern – character.

The headlamp clusters pointed to a new generation of lighting technology, the integrated units being equally praised and criticised for their adventurous design.

The interior was no less striking, with tortoise shell fittings complimenting the red leather and brushed aluminium.

While the name of the show car gave an indication of the engine layout – 'Boxster' is an ingenious combination of the words 'boxer' and 'roadster' – there was no engine specification available in 1993. None the less, for this Porsche to have anything other than a horizontally opposed engine was unthinkable. And almost inevitably, it had to be a 6-cylinder.

Using an existing powerplant wasn't practicable. The 911's veteran air-cooled engine was deemed unlikely to meet the noise and exhaust emissions requirements of several markets into the new century. So in a break with tradition, the new engine was water-cooled.

When the new car was revealed in late 1996, it had grown in size substantially. Porsche said this was just a question of practicality, that the show car's almost Lotus-like dimensions wouldn't meet ever more-demanding crash test regulations. It had to appeal to the widest possible market – a market that wasn't just populated by the die-hard Porsche fans.

It was also a fact that the Boxster shared a large proportion of its chassis components with the new 996, so a smaller car wasn't ever likely. Never the less, having teased everybody in

Dash layout of the Boxster shares many components with the 996 (and is much the better for it). Sat-nav is a very desirable option

1993 with the elegant proportions of the show car, the first impression of the final version (which was about 200mm, or 8 inches, longer) was something of a disappointment.

Another criticism was the starkness of the standard interior. Expanses of grained plastic was the order of the day, without a hint of the show car's tortoise shell details and little leather. But nobody disputed that the production design was more logical, practical and importantly, robust.

There was controversy over the naming of the car also. By calling it Boxster – the same as the show car – Porsche broke with a lifelong tradition of not using their own internal type numbers for their cars. In this case the Boxster was the Type 986 and many complained that this was the designation it should have had on its rear.

Time would prove the critics wrong however. The Boxster name would become as much a part of Porsche terminology as 911, 944 and 968.

What convinced everybody of the potential of the Boxster was the driving experience. With an all-aluminium, mid-mounted engine, the weight distribution was near-perfect and the dynamics of the car proved to be second to none.

Driving the Boxster proves the quality of its design, from the torsionally-stiff fully zinc-coated bodyshell, to its state-of-the-art suspension and braking system design.

Porsche's new roadster took the automobile world by storm and quickly became a very welcome best-seller for

Porsche. The Boxster was so successful that within a year, Porsche had agreed to sub-contract assembly to a Finnish company called Valmet, who would build Boxsters at a new facility in Uuisikaupunki. By the year 2000, and with demand for the 996 also exceeding all expectations, the majority of Boxsters were being assembled in Finland.

The Boxster had become a runaway success, saving the company from the economic ruin that it would otherwise have faced in the mid-1990s.

The new roadster had demonstrated the wisdom of widening the product line away from the traditional 911 and justified the decision to develop other brand new (and, in due course, far more radical) Porsche model lines.

To begin with, the only Boxster model was the 204bhp (150kW) 2.5-litre version, but in August 1999, the range divided into two new types. The new models were differentiated by engine size. The 220bhp (162kW) 2.7-litre Boxster replaced the 2.5-litre, while the 3.2-litre Boxster S took the model into a new position in the market.

As well as delivering 252bhp (185kW), the Boxster S was offered with uprated suspension and brakes.

The 'S' can be distinguished externally from the 2.7-litre Boxster by its third (central) inlet in the front bumper, its twin exhaust tailpipes and its cross-drilled brake discs with 4-piston 'Big Red' calipers.

The Boxster model range underwent another performance and cosmetic upgrade for the 2003 model year. For its seventh season, the 2.7-litre model was uprated to 228bhp (168kW), while the 'S' improved to

To improve driving comfort and safety, Porsche offered this attractive hardtop. The top can be removed (and stored in the garage) and the folding roof used in the normal way

1997 Boxster in Arena Red metallic

260bhp (191kW). These cars received a much-needed glass rear window and various other detail improvements.

A special Boxster S '550 Spyder' celebration model was introduced in late 2003, with an incresaed maximum power of 266bhp (196kW). These cars are identifiable by their unique GT-Silver paintwork.

At the Paris motor show in September 2004, an 80 per cent new Boxster was announced. Keeping the same engine capacities, the Boxster's maximum power increased to 240bhp (176kW), while the Boxster S improved to 280bhp (206kW). The second chapter in the Boxster story was only just starting.

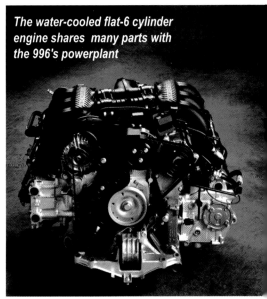

The water-cooled flat-6 cylinder engine shares many parts with the 996's powerplant

Model changes year by year

Bodyshell

The Boxster's bodyshell is an all-steel unitary construction made up of sheets that have been dipped in molten zinc. The zinc coating effectively galvanises the steel and in a process that Porsche have perfected over more than 25 years, gives the structure excellent life.

Porsche back their confidence in the bodyshell's longevity by offering a ten-year warranty against rust perforation. However to benefit from this, the car must have received annual check-ups from an official service centre and not have received any non-approved accident repairs.

The Boxster shares its structure forward of the door hinge posts with the 996. This includes the door shells. The front external panels (the bumper, and front wings) are unique. Since the Boxster is a mid-engine car (with the engine between the driver and the rear wheels), the whole of the rear of the car is also unique. The structure is very rigid and does not suffer unduly from the 'scuttle shake' that afflicts so many other open roadsters.

The mid-engine location is the ideal for a sports car because it has allowed the design engineers to develop a near-perfect 49 per cent front/51 per cent rear weight distribution on the front and rear axles. This layout also defines a strict 2-seater, but also permits two luggage areas: at the front (in front of the petrol tank) and at the rear (behind the engine).

These luggage areas also form the basis for the significant front and rear crash protection that the car offers. Additionally, the integrated design of the floorpan, with its substantial sill (rocker) panels, strengthened doors, windscreen frame and roll-over bar combine to make this Porsche one of the safest in a side impact or roll-over accident.

The styling of the Boxster is both modern, yet unmistakably this is a Porsche. The bonnet line recalls the 911, while other design cues acknowledge the racing Spyders of the 1950s. Nevertheless, the design of the front headlamps courted controversy at the car's launch. Today, these headlamps are accepted as just another part of the Boxster's appeal.

The Boxster has an electrically operated rear spoiler that extends at 75mph. It may not look much, but it is effective. At that speed aerodynamic drag is reduced by 4 per cent and lift over the rear axle is reduced by 40 per cent.

The Boxster has an electrically-operated convertible roof that deploys in approximately 12 seconds. To deploy the roof, the car must be stationary and with the hand-brake engaged.

The first cars used a single skin

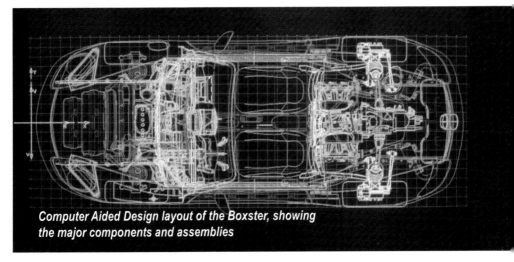

Computer Aided Design layout of the Boxster, showing the major components and assemblies

roof design, with a large, plastic rear window. This window allowed good rearwards visibility, but needed careful folding when the roof was stowed.

The 2000 Boxster S (2001 on the Boxster) received an improved double-skin roof, which reduced cabin noise, but unfortunately didn't do anything for the window folding problem. The big step forward came for the 2003 models with a full glass rear window. The downside was that rearwards visibility (particularly to the three-quarter areas) was reduced. These 2003 models received a restyled front bumper, side air vents and 'grey' rear light clusters.

Equipment and accessories

The most striking aspect of the Boxster's interior is the cluster of three round dials in front of the driver.

The round dials continue a Porsche tradition for simplicity in the dash layout and present the engine revolutions in the centre, speed (on the left) and a combination display of fuel level and coolant temperature (on the right). At the base of each dial is an LED panel that shows, from left to right: odometer, digital road speed and computer read-out (if this option is fitted) and time/engine oil level (the latter only before start).

Cars fitted with Tiptronic S automatic transmission also have a gear number indicator in the right-hand dial.

The standard 4-spoke steering wheel is adjustable for reach only (+/- 20mm or just under one inch) and contains the airbag and horn. The headlamp switch is on the lower dashboard, next to the ignition key slot on the outside of the

The analogue speedometer (on the left) isn't much use. Drivers quickly adapt to using the small digital read-out at its base

steering wheel. This outside position for the ignition dates from the time when races began with running 'Le Mans' style starts. A driver could leap into a Spyder and didn't have to grope around on the inside of the steering wheel looking for the starter.

Side impact airbags became standard on 2000 models, but were available as an option from the launch. POSIP (Porsche Side Impact Protection System) was the term used to describe the side airbag and energy absorbing design of the Boxster's doors. The new 'soft black' finish on the centre console, instrument panel details and door panels, combined with the new design of gear shift lever

and a strengthened design of centre console storage bin lid (with a strap to limit its travel) defines these 2000 models.

Porsche offer several different types of radio/CD systems for the Boxster (with a standard 6-speaker sound system) and there is a space in the front compartment for a CD changer. There is a double slot below the radio, which on most cars will be unused. However, these can accommodate the optional Porsche Communications Management (PCM) system. This unit combines mobile telephone, radio/CD and satellite navigation system.

The ancillary switches are

grouped around the top of the centre console and include traction control (if fitted), central locking, door mirror heating and convertible roof operation. The roof can only be opened when the handbrake is engaged.

The electrically-operated window switches are on the front of the central tunnel, next to the handbrake. This is also the switch location for the optional electrically-heated seats (if these are fitted). The adjuster for both of the electrically-operated external mirrors is mounted at the front of the driver's side window frame.

The seats are usually leather-faced and come as standard with basic manual adjustment for front-to-back and height, with electrical adjustment for back position. Later cars have full electrical operation and include adjustable lumbar support.

After age and condition, it is the accessories and options fitted that determine the desirability and value of any Boxster. The key options are discussed in the Buying section.

Interior

The standard early Boxster interior has moulded, grained plastic for the dash, door and other hard trim, with leather only used for the seat fronts. These early cars can look fairly bleak and as a result, examples with the full leather option hold their values better.

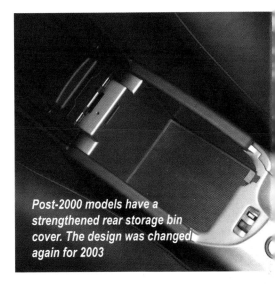

Post-2000 models have a strengthened rear storage bin cover. The design was changed again for 2003

'Full leather' includes the door trims, dash, centre console and roll-over bar, not just the seat facings. The option added roughly 10 per cent to the cost of the original car.

The 2000 model 2.7-litre Boxsters came with Alcantara (felt-effect) fabric for the seat facings, with what Porsche termed 'soft black' finished trim for the centre console, instrument panel and door trim. That year's Boxster S featured reverse-painted instrument dials, a 3-spoke airbag steering wheel and illuminated vanity mirrors in the sun visors. These cars also used the more attractive brushed aluminium finish for the gear lever and the compartment release levers.

The 2001 models (from August 2000) received an upgrade in the form of the dashboard layout used

Cockpit of a 1997 2.5-litre Boxster is fairly basic, but nevertheless very comfortable

on the 911 Turbo and better interior cockpit lighting. These models can be identified inside as the digital speedometer moved from the centre to the left hand dial and by the much smaller (electronic operation) front and rear compartment release switches.

If the Boxster's luggage capacity is very good in the front and rear, cabin storage for small items is somewhat limited. There are coat

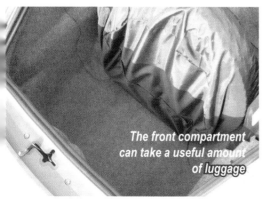

The front compartment can take a useful amount of luggage

hooks on the seat backs, but these are only usable if the seat is moved forward.

The centre console includes a small lockable rear box, while the doors each have storage compartments. There is another letterbox-size compartment behind the roll-over bar. The 2003 models gained a revised dashboard that included a full glovebox.

Engine

The all-aluminium, water-cooled 6-cylinder engine in the Boxster is mounted longitudinally behind a firewall, directly behind the seats.

The original Boxster has a 204bhp (150kW) 2.5-litre capacity, with a bore of 85.5mm and a stroke of 72mm. The capacity of the 220bhp (162kW) 2.7-litre cars was achieved by increasing the stroke to 78mm.

The 2000 model Boxster S offers a

maximum power of 252bhp (185kW), using a capacity of 3.2-litres. The stroke is the same as the 2.7-litre Boxster but the bore is increased in diameter to 93mm.

The cylinder heads have 4 valves per cylinder, these being driven by 2 overhead camshafts per bank (through hydraulic valve play adjusters).

The camshafts are driven by chains from an intermediate shaft that runs below the crankshaft (and is driven by it). The alloy cylinder block has liners that are cast in position. The forged steel crankshaft is supported by seven main bearings.

The Bosch Motronic M5.2 engine management system controls the sequential fuel injection, ignition and has anti-knock sensing (to permit use of a wide quality of unleaded gasoline types). The Motronic also controls the electrically-operated inlet camshaft timing adjustment (VarioCam), the optional traction control and the Automatic Brake Differential (ABD) systems. Motronic will act to block a spinning drive wheel by cutting back the power (traction control) and then by applying differential braking (ABD) on the affected wheel. This control was improved with the E-Gas throttle control (fly-by-wire) adopted on the 2.7-litre and Boxster S for the 2000 model year.

The Boxster uses dry sump lubrication, but with a separate oil tank integrated into the crankcase. An integrated water/oil heat exchanger helps with warm up and helps keep the lubricant cooler when the engine is hot. Another feature of the engine is that it uses a wholly plastic intake manifold.

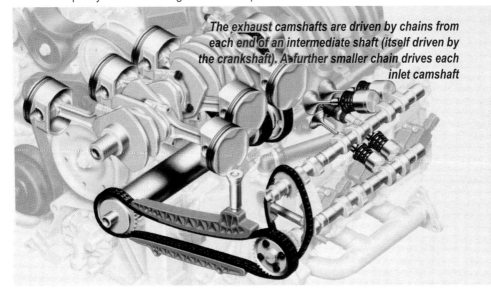

The exhaust camshafts are driven by chains from each end of an intermediate shaft (itself driven by the crankshaft). A further smaller chain drives each inlet camshaft

The flat-6 engine is mounted longitudinally in the chassis, with the clutch and gearbox to the rear

Bitte nicht berühren!
Please do not touch.

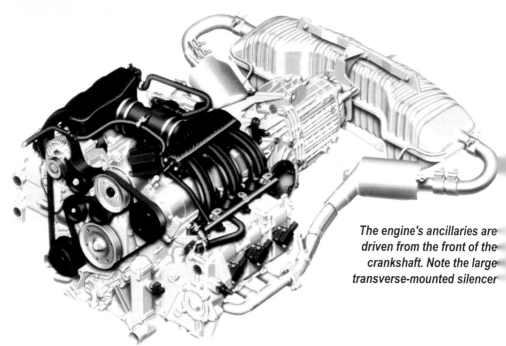

The engine's ancillaries are driven from the front of the crankshaft. Note the large transverse-mounted silencer

Transmission

The 2.5-litre and later 2.7-litre Boxster models use a 5-speed manual gearbox with a conventional 'H'-pattern gate layout, operated using a hydraulically-assisted dry plate clutch.

The Boxster S has a 6-speed gearbox. Many drivers new to the Boxster are surprised to learn that the car uses a cable-operated gear shift linkage. However, the shift action is an excellent and reliable solution (it is also used on the 996).

Tiptronic 'S' is also available for both models. On the Boxster, Tiptronic offers a full automatic and a conventional two-pedal P-R-N-1-2-3-4-D operation. By moving the lever over to the right and into a separate front-back gate, gears can be changed by 'tipping' (hence the name) the lever forwards or backwards. The 'S' designation refers to the addition of Tiptronic shift buttons on the steering wheel.

Tiptronic is an intelligent shift design and will block manual shifts at the wrong engine or road speeds. With this facility, it can also be used to pre-select ratios.

Suspension and steering

The Boxster's front suspension uses the MacPherson principle, with a single, offset and rising rate conical spring over each Bilstein telescopic shock absorber. The wheel is stabilised by a cast alloy lower control arm and an anti-roll bar.

The rear suspension is also based on the MacPherson principle with a

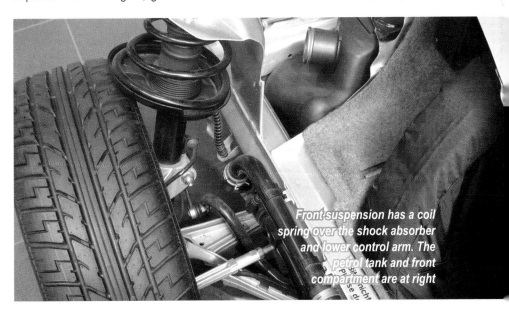

Front suspension has a coil spring over the shock absorber and lower control arm. The petrol tank and front compartment are at right

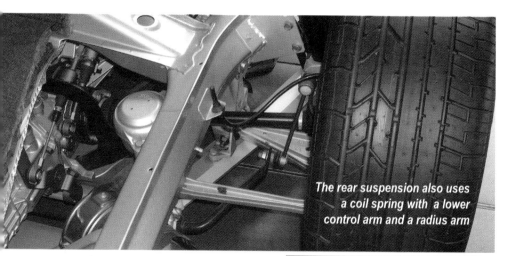

The rear suspension also uses a coil spring with a lower control arm and a radius arm

conventional coil spring, using a single lower control arm, a lateral (radius) arm and an anti-roll bar. The rear suspension components are supported by an aluminium rear sub-frame under the gearbox.

The power-assisted rack and pinion steering operates through an articulated (and therefore safer) steering column.

Brakes, wheels and tyres

The dual circuit, hydraulic braking system on the standard Boxster uses ventilated, steel disc brakes. The disc sizes are 298mm (11.7 inches) diameter on the front axle and 292mm (11.5 inches) on the rear. The 4-piston 'black' calipers are by Brembo. Antilock Braking System (ABS) is standard on the Boxster.

The Boxster S uses the drilled and ventilated steel discs from the 996, with the 4-piston 'Big Red' calipers first fitted

to the 911 Turbo. These discs are fitted to the 2003 2.7-litre models.

There have been several wheel types offered for the Boxster. The standard early fit to the 2.5-litre Boxster were 16-inch cast alloy wheels (with a 'split' 5-spoke design) in sizes 6J and 7J. Optionally available were 17-inch 7J and 8.5J alloy wheels in a 2-piece 'Sport Classic' 10-spoke design. The optional 17-inch 'Turbo-look' design – a 5-spoke wheel that looked as if the centres had spun slightly ahead of the rims – was offered from 1998.

For those wanting a really firm ride there were 7.5J x 18 front and 9J x 18 rear wheels on offer in the 2-piece 'Sport Design' (BBS-type multi-spoke) design.

The Boxster S came with 17-inch wheels as standard, with the 18-inch rims as an option.

Wheel gallery: Opposite page middle: The first Boxsters were fitted with these 16-inch 5-spoke cast alloy wheels. Below is the stylish 5-spoke wheel that served as the early 17-inch option. This page (top left) is the 1999-onwards optional 17-inch Turbo-look alloy. The Sport Classic (top right) and 10-spoke Sport Design (middle right) are 2-piece 18-inch options. The Carrera-style 18-inch alloy was a later option for the Boxster

The brake discs on the 2.5litre Boxsters are not cross-drilled

The 2.5-litre Boxster has 205/55ZR16 section front tyres as standard with 205/50ZR17 for the optional 17-inch wheels. For the 18-inch front wheels the wider, lower profile 225/40ZR18 tyres are fitted. These front tyres sizes are the same for the 2.7-litre Boxster, with only the 17- and 18-inch sizes being used on the 'S.'

The standard rear tyres on a 2.5-litre model are 225/50ZR16, increasing to 255/40ZR17 or 265/35ZR18. The tyre sizes stay the same for the 17- and 18-inch wheels used on the later models.

The cross-drilled and ventilated steel discs on the Boxster S have 4-piston 'Big Red' calipers

*The Boxster '550 Anniversary
in GT-Silver metallic*

Special models

2004 Boxster S '550 anniversary'

This special Boxster S was produced from March 2004 to celebrate the 50th anniversary of the 550 Spyder. It was finished in GT Silver (first used on the limited edition Carrera GT) with silver-painted side grilles and silvered rear logo. The convertible roof came in dark brown 'Cocoa' colour, or, if dark grey leather was specified for the interior, black. The brake calipers were finished in silver and a stainless steel exhaust was fitted. 18-inch wheels with Seal Grey centres were used, with 5mm spacers all round.

The special interior included a limited edition plate on the centre console and a short-throw gear shift. The seat backs, centre console, roll-over bar and dash details were painted in GT-Silver. Heated seats, air conditioning, the Porsche CDR-23 CD/radio, Litronic headlamps and headlamp washers were standard.

The ride height was reduced by 10mm, with firmer suspension. This special Boxster also has Porsche Stability Management (PSM). PSM is the collective name given to the traction control system that includes the E-gas throttle and differential antilock braking).

The 3.2-litre engine delivered a maximum power of 266bhp (196kW), up 6bhp on the standard car. Maximum torque was unchanged. Top speed rose 2mph while 0 to 62mph acceleration remained the same.

The 2005 Boxsters

A new generation

An 80 per cent new Boxster model range was announced at the Paris motor show in September 2004, for the 2005 model year. The new cars represented a major upgrade in the appearance and specification.

Given the internal type number 987, the second generation Boxsters were heavily revised in all areas, although in outward appearance they looked much the same.

The Boxster range made another major step forward in January 2005, when a new coupe model was announced. The coupe brought a new diversity to the Boxster offering, with Porsche confident that the car woiuld not challenge the existing position of the 911 Carrera.

After eight years of spectacular success, when more than 160,000 examples were sold, Porsche maintained there was little need to change a formula that had been so successful first time around. Boxster buyers, they believed, occupied a diffeent market segment to buyers of the higher priced 911 models - hence the new coupe. The new Boxster was said to share only 30-40 per cent of its parts with the 997, significantly less than the first generation car and the 996.

But in true Porsche style, the new Boxsters were significantly changed in detail. This was no minor facelift, but a major makeover. This difference is an important one for buyers thinking about whether to buy a first or second generation model. The changes are far greater than those made for instance on the 2000 or the 2003 models.

The 2005 Boxster was slightly wider (the front track is greater by 24mm and the rear track by 35mm) and this, combined with more flared wings and revised front and rear bumpers, combined to give the new car a

This Guards Red Boxster S (below) has 19-inch wheels, which are really only a practical proposition with the PASM package. The original Porsche factory buildings in Gmünd, Austria (left) make a suitable backdrop for this Speed Yellow Boxster S

General arrangement (above) of the new Boxster echoes the first generation cars. Undertray (left) is all new.

Porsche Active Suspension Management (PASM) brought a new level of handling confidence to the Boxster

sharper, more aggressive appearance.

The openings in the front and sides were larger and were given a more chiselled look, while the new headlamps took a styling lead from the early 1960s racing Porsches.

There were new, Carrera GT-style exterior mirrors and larger, more square roll-over bars. The side windows were also reprofiled to make entry easier.

The underbody was fully covered and this helped reduce the drag coefficient from 0.31 to 0.29 on the Boxster, and from 0.32 to 0.30 on the S.

The engine and transmisssion received considerable work to improve relibality and the service interval moved out to 18,000 miles (from 12,000 miles). Capacities remain at 2.7-litres for the Boxster and 3.2-litres for the Boxster S. Maximum power for the 2.7 was 240bhp (176kW), up 12bhp (8kW). The S version improved by 20bhp (15kW) to a maximum 280bhp (191kW).

The improved performance came from a new twin chamber intake system and a larger

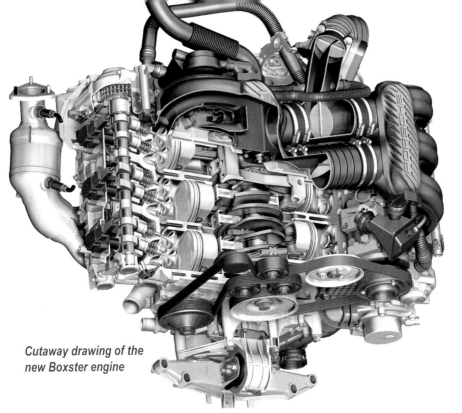

Cutaway drawing of the new Boxster engine

capacity exhaust system. Both changes also significantly improved the torque at lower rpm. Maximum torque for the Boxster was now 270Nm (199lb.ft) from 4700-6000rpm, while the S delivered a maximum torque of 320Nm (236lb.ft) over the same rpm range.

Engine reliability is an issue on some first generation Boxsters. The new crankshaft has been lightened in the area of the flywheel/rear main seal overhang, which should improve the reliability of the seal. Using much improved vendor quality control, Porsche are also convinced they are on top of any reliability issues with the casting of the crankcase.

The other big engine reliability improvement concerns the new moulded technique used for the poly-rib belt at the front of the engine, which should extend its life considerably.

While the 5-speed gearbox in the Boxster was improved, an all-new 6-speed gearbox was introduced for the S. The shift action became altogether shorter and crisper. Both

The new 6-speed gearbox for the Boxster S. Exhaust system on both models has a larger capacity and improves power

The second generation Boxster benefits from eight years of production development. Note 17-inch Boxster 2 alloy wheels on this GT-Silver Boxster

cars were available with 5-speed Tiptronic S automatic transmission.

The second generation Boxster offered superior driving dynamics and crash safety. The Boxster offered a lighter, stiffer conventional suspension (with the usual coil spring/damper layout), combined with a power-assisted, variable rate (depending on road speed) steering.

The new Boxsters came with a new version of Porsche Stability Management (PSM), an active safety package that transforms the driving characteristics near the handling limits. PSM manages the ABS, traction control (Anti-spin control or ASC), engine drag control (EDC) and the automatic brake differential (ABD), with many features only previously seen on the 911. PSM works only at speeds less than 50mph and the system can be switched off if desired.

The new version is less intrusive and more progressive. It doesn't simply take over the brake and throttle control when a wheel loses traction.

The basic PSM could be enhanced with Porsche Active Suspension Management (PASM). Ride height on cars fitted with this option was 10mm lower and the system incorporated what Porsche termed adaptive dampers to soften or harden the dampers as required.

The 'intelligent' control system compares

The new door trims included window lifters relocated next to the door handle

The Sport Chrono package came with this dash-mounted stopwatch

PCCB brakes were an option on the new Boxsters

The 19-inch Carrera S alloy wheel. This Boxster S has the yellow calipers of the PCCB system

the data emitted by two accelerometers fitted to the tops of the front-right and rear-left dampers to the car's lateral acceleration, steering angle, road speed, brake pressure and engine torque. The control unit then determines the optimum damper control mapping and adjusts the damper's response on each wheel as necessary. The driver can choose between two suspension control programmes: Normal for everyday driving and Sport for faster driving.

The PASM is a very desirable extra on any Boxster, but almost essential for cars fitted with 19-inch wheels. The ride with these big wheels on conventional suspension is harsh, particularly if the car is used everyday. The PASM softens the damper response considerably and makes these wheels a realistic proposition for regular street use (but mind the rims on high kerbs!).

The Sport Chrono package was a further option for cars with PASM. This package provides a steeper accelerator pedal control map, an abrupt cut-off at higher revolutions and a harder intervention with PASM near the car's adhesion limits. The package is a nice extra on a used Boxster, although the stopwatch on the dash is something of a decoration. The real value of this option is that it alows the driver the back-off the superb, new generation Porsche Stability Management (PSM) and get some movement out of the car during fast driving.

The brakes were upgraded on both models, with larger discs on the rear axles. Both models now offered cross-drilled, ventilated cast-iron discs as standard. The calipers were colour-coded as before – black for the Boxster and red for the S.

For the first time Boxsters were offered with the Porsche Ceramic Composite Brake (PCCB) option. These brakes offer lower unsprung weight and improved braking efficiency under extreme conditions.

Because of the replacement costs associated with the ceramic components (the discs and their pads), it is my opinion that Boxsters fitted with these brakes are not practical for general street use.

The interior of the new Boxsters was all-new. The dash and console mouldings used 'slush' technology for a more attractive finish (than the previous, rather basic, moulded plastic look). The dash featured new, round fresh air vents and the steering wheel could be adjusted for height as well as reach.

Four seat options were available and all were mounted lower in the car to improve comfort for the taller driver.

The standard seats offered electrical adjustment of the backrest, the first option offered adjustment of all positions and lumbar support, while the second option was the leather Sports seat with better side support. The third option was an adaptive Sports seat with adjustment of the side supports at the bottom and in the backrest.

The new Boxsters also came with a new head airbag fitted within the sills of each door. These combined with the thorax airbags in the seat backrests and the conventional frontal airbags.

The electric roof could be opened or closed up to a speed of 30mph.

The new Boxster was offered with an optional Sports steering wheel and also a multi-function steering wheel for use with the (also optional) Porsche Communications Management (PCM) system. The PCM offered the usual radio/CD/telephone installation with, for the first time, a DVD-based satellite navigation system. The six steering wheel buttons allowed the driver to control these functions. Another desirable in-car option was the Bose Surround Sound 11-speaker system.

PASM has brought new confidence to the second Boxster generation

The chassis number is found in several places around the car, including this label on the driver's door catch post

Boxster production information (1997 to 2005)

Model types and chassis numbers
The following information is derived from a number of sources and serves to clarify the basic models and their model years.

Table notes
The first models listed for each year are those specified for Germany and Rest of World (RoW) markets, followed by the specific models for the USA (abbreviated to US).

The chassis numbers shown are industry standard 17-character Vehicle Identification Numbers (VIN). To illustrate what they mean, consider this typical US Boxster: WPOCA298_XS600001. WPO is the world make code for Porsche; CA2 is the US VSD code. The first VSD letter is the body type – C is for a Cabriolet. The second VSD letter is the engine/transmission type – A for 2-wheel drive (B is for 4-wheel drive). The third VSD digit is the occupant safety system type – 0 for seat belts only, 1 for driver airbag, 2 for driver/passenger airbags. In other markets (like Europe) these three VSD characters are just left ZZZ (eg: WPOZZZ98ZXS6000061). Next in the chassis number are the first two digits of the model type (98) followed by a test number (on US models this NHTSA space is usually left blank and in RoW it's left as a Z) and the model year letter (V for 1997, W for 1998, X for 1999, Y for 2000). The model year letter changed to 1 in 2001, then 2 for 2002 etc. The 11th digit is the plant code: S for Stuttgart or U for Uuisikaupunki; next is the third digit of the type number (6) and the body/engine code. The last 4 digits are the serial number. The 3rd digit of the engine number also corresponds with the model year letter eg: 65X00001 is a 1999 model.

The first 60 chassis numbers for each model are reserved for Porsche internal use.

Model	Borexstroke (mm)	Capacity (cc)	BHP (kW) (DIN, max)	Chassis number series
1997				
Boxster	85.5x72	2480	204 (150)	WPOZZZ98ZVS600001-
Boxster US	85.5x72	2480	204 (150)	WPOCA298_VS600001-
1998				
Boxster	85.5x72	2480	204 (150)	WPOZZZ98ZWS600001-
Boxster US	85.5x72	2480	204 (150)	WPOCA298_WS600001-
1999				
Boxster	85.5x72	2480	204 (150)	WPOZZZ98ZXS600001-
Boxster US	85.5x72	2480	204 (150)	WPOCA298_XS600001-
2000				
Boxster	85.5x78	2687	220 (162)	WPOZZZ98ZYS600001-
Boxster S	93x78	3179	252 (185)	WPOZZZ98ZYS640001-
Boxster US	85.5x78	2687	220 (162)	WPOCA298_YS600001-
Boxster S US	93x78	3179	252 (185)	WPOCA298_YS600001-
2001				
Boxster	85.5x78	2687	220 (162)	WPOZZZ98Z1S600001-
Boxster S	93x78	3179	252 (185)	WPOZZZ98Z1S640001-
Boxster US	85.5x78	2687	220 (162)	WPOCA298_1S600001-
Boxster S US	93x78	3179	252 (185)	WPOCA298_1S640001-
2002				
Boxster	85.5x78	2687	220 (162)	WPOZZZ98Z2S600001-
Boxster S	93x78	3179	252 (185)	WPOZZZ98Z2S640001-
Boxster US	85.5x78	2687	220 (162)	WPOCA298_2S600001-
Boxster S US	93x78	3179	252 (185)	WPOCA298_2S640001-
2003				
Boxster	85.5x78	2687	228 (168)	WPOZZZ98Z3S600001-
Boxster S	93x78	3179	260 (191)	WPOZZZ98Z3S640001-
Boxster US	85.5x78	2687	228 (168)	WPOCA298_3S600001-
Boxster S US	93x78	3179	260 (191)	WPOCA298_3S640001-
2004				
Boxster	85.5x78	2687	228 (168)	WPOZZZ98Z4S600001-
Boxster S	93x78	3179	260 (191)	WPOZZZ98Z4S640001-
Boxster US	85.5x78	2687	228 (168)	WPOCA298_4S600001-
Boxster S US	93x78	3179	260 (191)	WPOCA298_4S640001-
Boxster S 550	93x78	3179	266 (196)	WPOZZZ98Z4S640001-
2005				
Boxster	85.5x78	2687	240 (176)	WPOZZZ98Z5U700001-
Boxster S	93x78	3179	280 (206)	WPOZZZ98Z5U720001-
Boxster US	85.5x78	2687	240 (176)	WPOCA298_4U700001-
Boxster S US	93x78	3179	280 (206)	WPOCA298_4U720001-

The second generation Boxster, produced from October 2004, is known internally at Porsche as the Type 987. As far as can be established nearly all Boxster production is planned for the Finland manufacturing location

Year by year body colours and interior choices (1996-2005)

This section lists the bodyshell and roof colour choices (including special order colours) and fabrics available from year to year.

1997

Standard external body colours

Black, Guards Red, Pastel Yellow, Glacier White Special colours: Ocean Blue metallic, Zenith blue metallic, Arena red metallic, Arctic silver metallic, Ocean jade metallic, Black metallic

Fabrics/carpets: Leather, leatherette or 'Dunes' cloth in Black, Graphite grey, Savanna (tan), Metropole blue. Special colours in Nephrite green and Boxster red (both with black roof)

Roof colours

Black, Graphite grey, Metropole blue

1998

Standard external body colours

Black, Guards red, Pastel yellow, Glacier white Special colours: Ocean blue metallic, Zenith blue metallic, Arena red metallic, Arctic silver metallic, Ocean jade metallic, Black metallic

Fabrics/carpets: Leather, leatherette or 'Dunes' cloth in Black, Graphite grey, Savanna (tan), Metropole blue. Special colours in Nephrite green and Boxster red (both with black roof)

Roof colours

Black, Graphite grey, Metropole blue

1999

Standard external body colours

Black, Guards Red, Pastel Yellow, Glacier White Special colours: Ocean Blue Metallic, Zenith Blue Metallic, Arena Red Metallic, Arctic Silver Metallic, Ocean Jade Metallic, Black Metallic

Fabrics/carpets: Leather, leatherette or 'Dunes' cloth in Black, Graphite Grey, Savanna (tan), Metropole Blue. Special colours in Nephrite Green and Boxster Red (both with black roof)

Roof colours

Black, Graphite Grey, Metropole Blue

2000

Standard external body colours

Black, Guards Red, Biarritz White, Speed Yellow Special colours: Ocean Blue Metallic, Zenith Blue Metallic, Arena Red Metallic, Arctic Silver Metallic, Ocean Jade Metallic, Black Metallic

Fabrics/carpets: Leather, leatherette or 'Dunes' cloth in Black, Graphite Grey, Savanna (tan), Metropole Blue. Special colours in Nephrite Green and Boxster Red (both with black roof)

Roof colours: Black, Graphite Grey, Metropole Blue

2001

Standard exterior colours

Black, Guards red, Biarritz white, Speed yellow

Metallic exterior colours: Black metallic, Lapis blue metallic, Rain Forest Green metallic, Orient Red metallic, Arctic Silver metallic, Seal Grey metallic, Meridian metallic, Zanzibar Red

Fabrics/carpets

Leather, Leatherette, Alcantara fabric in Black, Graphite Grey, Savanna (tan), Metropole Blue, Nephrite Green. Special interior colours: Boxster Red, Cinnamon Brown. Natural leather in Grey or Brown

Roof colours

Black, Graphite grey, Metropole blue

2002

Standard exterior colours

Black, Guards Red, Biarritz White, Speed Yellow

Metallic exterior colours: Black Metallic, Lapis Blue Metallic, Rainforest Green Metallic, Orient Red Metallic, Arctic Silver Metallic, Seal Grey Metallic, Meridian Metallic, Zanzibar Red

Roof colours

Black, Graphite Grey, Metropole Blue

Fabrics/carpets

Leather, Leatherette, Alcantara fabric in Black, Graphite Grey, Savanna (tan), Metropole Blue, Nephrite Green. Special interior colours: Boxster Red, Cinnamon Brown. Natural leather in Grey or Brown

2003

Standard exterior colours

Black. Carrara White, Guards Red, Speed Yellow

Metallic exterior colours: Carmon Red metallic, Atlas Grey metallic, Midnight Blue metallic, Dark Teal metallic, Lapis Blue metallic, Arctic Silver metallic, Seal Grey metallic, Basalt Black metallic.

Special body colours

Forest Green metallic, Cobalt Blue metallic, Polar Silver metallic, Slate Grey metallic, Meridian metallic.

Roof colours

Black, Graphite Grey, Metropole blue

Fabrics

Leather, Leatherette and Alcantara fabrics (for seat centres) in Black, Graphite Grey, Metropole Blue and Savanna (tan)

2004

Standard exterior colours

Black, Carrara White, Guards red, Speed Yellow

Metallic exterior colours Carmon Red metallic, Atlas Grey metallic, Midnight Blue metallic, Dark Teal metallic, Lapis Blue metallic, Arctic Silver metallic, Seal Grey metallic, Basalt Black metallic.

Special body colours

Forest green metallic, Cobalt blue metallic, Polar silver metallic, Slate grey metallic, Meridian metallic. For 550 anniversary model: GT-Silver metallic

Roof colours:

Black, Graphite grey, Metropole blue

Fabrics/carpets: Leather, Leatherette and Alcantara fabrics (for seat centres) in Black, Graphite brey, Metropole blue and Savanna (tan)

2005 (Second generation)

Standard exterior colours

Black. Carrara white, Guards red, Speed yellow.

Metallic exterior colours: Carmon red metallic, Atlas Grey metallic, Lagoon Green metallic, Lapis Blue metallic, Arctic Silver metallic, Seal Grey metallic, Basalt Black metallic, Dark Olive metallic.

Special body colours

Forest Green metallic, Cobalt Blue metallic, Slate grey metallic, GT-Silver metallic

Roof colours

Black, Stone Grey, Metropole blue

Fabrics/carpets: Partial leather in Black, Palm Green, Sand Beige, Ocean Blue.

Full leather in Black, Palm Green, Sand Beige, Stone Grey. Sports seats in leather: Black, Ocean Blue, Stone Grey, Palm Green, Sand Beige. Natural leather in Drak Grey, Cocoa, Terracotta, Natural Brown.

Boxster option codes 1996-2004

General
TD4 Tourist delivery programme

Chassis
030 Sports chassis
395 16-inch alloy wheel
396 17-inch Boxster Design wheels and tyres
413 18-inch Turbo-Look wheels
446 Wheel centres with coloured Porsche crest
P37/222 Traction control with Active Brake Differential
TT3/249 Tiptronic transmission
197 Stronger battery
224 Automatic limited slip differential
481 5-speed manual gearbox
492 Preparation for left-hand traffic
562 Driver and passenger airbag system
566 Foglamps, clear
567 Top-tint windscreen

Exterior
261 Exterior mirror, plain, left
270 Exterior mirror, plain, right
271 Exterior mirror, spherical surface, left
288 Headlight washers
498 Deleted model designation
551 Wind deflector
550 Hard top in body colour incl heated rear window
549 Roof transport system
635 Park assist
601 Litronic headlights

Interior
139 Heated seat, left
340 Heated seat, right
E51 Large leather dashboard package
E52 Small leather dashboard package
E53 Large mahogany dashboard package
E54 Small mahogany dashboard package
E55 Large carbon dashboard package
E56 Small carbon dashboard package

274 Vanity mirrors, illuminated
320 Radio Porsche CR11
326 Radio Porsche CR21
329 Cassette radio Porsche CR210
330 radio Porsche CR31
421 Cassette compartment in centre console
424 CD shelf in centre console
432 Tiptronic S steering wheel
436 3-spoke steering wheel
441 Prepared for radio installation
454 Cruise control
465 Rear foglamp, left
466 Rear foglamp, right
490 6-speaker Hi-Fi sound system
509 Fire extinguisher
513 Lumbar support, right side
531 Immobiliser, central locking system
534 Alarm
535 Remote controlled alarm system
536 Alarm siren and movement sensor
539 Manual height adjustment, left side
540 Manual height adjustment, right side
571 Activated charcoal filter
573 Air conditioning
580 Non-smoking package
586 Lumbar support, left side
006 Floormats
659 On Board Computer
662 Porsche Communications Management
686 Radio Porsche CDR21
688 Radio Porsche CDR210
692 Remote CD changer
696 AM/FM Radio with CD player
982 Ruffled leather seats

Porsche Exclusive
An additional selection of factory fitted options was available through the Porsche Exclusive range. Porsche Exclusive is the factory's own customisation business. Porsche Tequipment is a separate range of after-market products that could be fitted after purchase of the car.
What follows is just a sample of a large selection.
X21 Telephone console in leather

X26 Leather 4-spoke airbag steering wheel
X45 Instrument dials painted in interior colour
X68 Tonneau cover in roof colour
X69 Carbon door sills
X70 Stainless steel doors sills
X71 Aluminium-look instrument dials
X77 Carbon/leather 4-spoke airbag steering wheel
X89 Wheel centres coloured to customer sample
XAA Boxster aerokit, with front and rear spoiler, sill panels
XAB Speedster rear, in body colour
XD3 Rain sensor
XE3 Auto-dimming rear view mirror
XJB Centre console painted in body colour
XLA Exhaust pipe
XME Painted rear centre console
XMF Leather front centre console
XMH Roll-over bar covers in leather
XMJ Carbonfibre rear centre console
XMK Roll-over bar painted in body colour
XML Roll-over bar in chrome finish
XMR Leather sunvisors
XMU Mahogany/Aluminum/Leather gear shift knob and handbrake grip
XMW Mahogany/Aluminum/Leather Tiptronic shift lever and handbrake grip
XMY Arctic silver painted roll-over bar
XMZ Leather rear centre console
XN3 Airbag steering wheel with wood/leather
XNE Airbag steering wheel with mahogany/ aluminium rivets/leather
XNG Lower part of instrument panel covered with leather
XNJ Leather speaker covers
XNN Leather centre air vents
XNS Leather steering column
XNT Mahogany/Leather 4-spoke airbag steering wheel
XPA 3-spoke Sports steering wheel with leather rim
XPD 3-spoke Sports steering wheel with carbonfibre rim
XRA 17-inch Sport Classic wheels and tyres

XRB 18-inch Sport Classic wheels and tyres
XRH 17-inch Dyno wheels and tyres
XRL 18-inch Sport Design (10-spoke) wheels and tyres
XRK 18-inch Turbo-look wheels
XD9 Painted Rims
XSA Sports seats, left and right with painted seat backs
XSC Embossed headrests
XSD Leather seat adjustment knobs
XTC Leather and silver door interior
XTG Leather panels by door
XX2 Footwell lighting
Y03 Carbon/leather gear lever knob and handbrake grip
Y06 Aluminum/Leather Gear shift Knob and handbrake grip
Y23 Aluminum/Leather Tiptronic shift lever and handbrake grip
Y24 Carbonfibre Tiptronic shift lever and handbrake grip
Z100 Deviating carpet colour
Z102 Deviating seatbelt colour
Z103 Deviating seat stitching colour
Z104 Boxster red or Nephrite green leather seats
Z105 Deviating leather seat colour
Z106 Deviating door panel stitching colour

Option packages
P14 Heated front seat package, left and right
P15 Full electric seats with memory
P16 Sport package with 396, 551, 454, 535, 692, 659, X71, XML, Y23, X70, XLA
P17 Sport Touring package with 396, 551, 490, 454, 535, 692, 659, X71, XML, Y23, X70, XLA
P18 Sport Touring package with 396, 551, 490, 454, 535, 692, 659, X71 XML, Y23, X70, XLA
P38 Stiffer springs, shock absorbers and anti-roll bars, 396, P37
P49 Digital Sound Processing package
P63 Sports package with 396, 551, 490, 454, 535, 688
P64 Sport touring package with 396, 551, 490,

454, 535, 692, 659, X71, XML, Y23, X70, XLA

P65 Sport Touring package with 396, 551, 490, 454, 535, 692, 659, X71, XML, Y23, X70, XLA

P69 Sport Design package

P77 Leather Sports seats with manual reach adjustment and electric backrest

P84 Sport package as P63 but with XRA 17-inch Sport Classic wheels

P85 Sport touring package as P64 but with XRA 17-inch Sport Classic wheels

P86 Sport touring package as P65 but with XRA 17-inch Sport Classic wheels

'Trend' package includes: Ocean Jade metallic or Zenith Blue metallic paint. Details painted in Graphite Grey include (interior trim around windscreen/windows, instrument rings, top of gear lever, door tube, roll-over bar).

Details painted in roof colour (switch and instrument panel, door trim, lid of centre console storage bin, side panels of centre console, hood, all-cloth seats).

'Sport Design' package includes: Black, diamond-pattern finish on instrument panel, door trim and centre console side panels. Black roof, Sports seats, 3 spoke steering wheel. Items painted in metallic grey include: lower part of instrument panel, switch trim, trim around central air vent, door opener cover, door tube, instrument

rings, lids to door storage bins, centre console, including hand-brake lever, top of gear lever, roll-over bar. Details in black leather: instrument panel, cover for passenger airbag, lid of centre console storage bin, covering of roll-over bar, sports seats, 3-spoke steering wheel

Sport package includes:

Leather seats, traction control, wind deflector, 17-inch wheels, ride height lowered 10mm, stiffened springs and anti-roll bars, stiffer shock absorbers

Classic package includes:

Metallic paint, leather seats, graphite grey interior paint with amber details

Convenience package (USA) includes:

CD shelf in centre console, 6-speaker sound system, cruise control, coloured crests on wheels, remote alarm, wind stop (deflector)

Convenience package Plus (USA) includes:

As above plus Porsche Stability Management (PSM), trip computer, Bose (equalisation and 10-speaker) sound system, Litronic headlamps

Lux package (UK) includes:

Leather seats, 17-inch wheels, wind deflector, air conditioning, on-board computer

The option codes are shown on the Vehicle Identification Label (VIL) under the bonnet and on page 4 of the Guarantee & Maintenance booklet

The second generation Boxsters were 80 per cent new. This is a Boxster S in Arctic Silver, with 19-inch wheels and PCCB brakes (with yellow calipers)

Boxster S

Buying a used Boxster

The Boxster has established an enviable record of reliability and low depreciation in every marketplace in which it has appeared. This is a car that many owners use every day, rather than as a third car for weekends. As a result mileages can typically average 10-12,000 miles a year or more. As long as the car is regularly and properly serviced, such a history should not be a problem. As we will discuss, the value of the car is dependent as much on its colour and quality of options as its year and condition.

There are some basic rules that apply to buying any used car. You won't remember all these words when you go to see cars, but the most important rule is not to buy on impulse.

If you like a car, but the checking bores you, get an expert to do that. It could save you thousands on either repair bills or when you come to sell it. If you have to put a holding deposit on a car you like, keep it as small as possible. Many dealers will refuse to refund a deposit if you change your mind.

This section will go into greater detail on the areas of the car that must be checked out before sale, to lessen the risk of heartbreak later on. We'll start with what to look for in the car's documentation.

Documentation

A Boxster is a complex machine and so it's important that the car you buy comes with a full and comprehensive service history. Nevertheless, it is quite normal that cars more than three or four years old may not have a recent history with an Official Porsche Centre.

Many owners look for better value than the official network can offer, but if this is the route taken, it is essential the independent specialist chosen has the experience and the specific computer equipment to service the car properly.

On page 4 of the Guarantee & Maintenance book the date of first registration and the stamp of the supplying official dealer should be shown alongside the Vehicle Identification Label (VIL). The data on this label will agree with the chassis number data shown on the car itself. If any part of this data is missing or non-specific, be on guard.

The service stamps begin on page 16 of this book and should show how regularly the car has been serviced. Be wary if the stamps appear all the same, written by the same hand and by the same pen! Look for long gaps that suggest irregular servicing. The best security for these service stamps is a healthy file of receipts and service reports to back up the book. In particular, look for evidence of major (in other words, expensive) work such as a new clutch or even an engine rebuild. Also, look for receipts for smaller items – a conscientious owner will have meticulously kept every single receipt in age-order and such a collection builds up into a useful picture of a car's life.

The same conscientious owner will also have kept all the car's MoT certificates (in the UK), which are invaluable in helping to verify mileage. Each certificate has the car's chassis number and mileage at the time of the test shown on it, so you should be able to spot any discrepancies. This can be cross-referenced with mileages written on service invoices. Note, though, that any

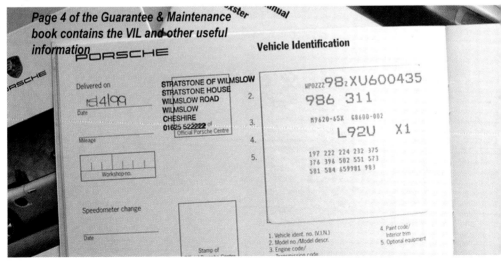

Page 4 of the Guarantee & Maintenance book contains the VIL and other useful information

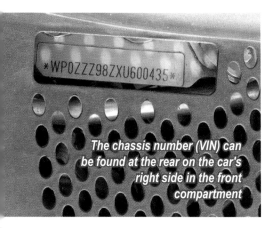

The chassis number (VIN) can be found at the rear on the car's right side in the front compartment

The VIN is also visible behind the lower left side of the windscreen

The engine number is on the engine underside, at the right rear of the sump cover. It isn't always as readable as this!

form of paperwork can be faked, so look out for photocopied invoices and make sure that they show the correct registration or chassis number.

Also, don't forget to check the car's statutory documentation (registration document V5 in the UK) – and be wary of a seller who doesn't have this paperwork. Always cross-check the chassis number shown on the registration document with that on the car itself.

In the UK you can check if a UK-registered car has any outstanding finance, has been declared an insurance write-off, or has a police history by going to the HPI website at www.hpicheck.com. Other countries have equivalent resources.

At the end of the day, though, as welcome as a full and comprehensive history is, it can never tell the whole story. Just because a car has been well-looked after in the past doesn't automatically mean it's a good buy now. It could be being sold because the owner received a nasty shock at the last service and some expensive work is due.

Bodyshell

One of the first things to check is the car's chassis number. This is stamped onto the car in four easily-checked places – at the foot of the windscreen on the left side, in the front compartment by the battery and on the VIL label under the bonnet. It is also shown on the plate in the driver's door catch post. Check that this number corresponds with the car's model and year and also with the vehicle's official documentation.

If the numbers are not correct, then ask the vendor why, and be very wary if they don't come up with a satisfactory explanation. If the VIL label under the bonnet or that by the driver's door is missing, then it suggests there have been accident damage repairs.

Only very low mileage cars are likely to have had no cosmetic repainting at all, so don't be put off if you find evidence of such work (as long as it is to a good standard). The front bumper, bonnet and exterior mirrors are vulnerable to stone chips and so many cars will have had these areas resprayed at some point. Indeed, this can be a sign of a well-looked after car and is preferable to chips that have been touched-up with a brush (although even this is preferable to nothing at all, which can lead to corrosion).

What is important, though, is that any such paintwork rectification has been undertaken to a high standard and that the new paint blends well with the old (for colour and finish). Look over the bodyshell very carefully for any signs of a non-factory

More often than not, it is likely used Boxsters of any age will have received some form of cosmetic paintwork rectification

finish (which might include dents, scrapes, trapped contamination under the paint and overspray). And of course, do this outside, during daylight and not in the rain.

As we have already discussed, the Boxster has a fully galvanised bodyshell and the best cars under 10 years old will have an intact official warranty against rust perforation. To have this there must be a full official service history, with page 21 of the Guarantee & Maintenance book fully stamped to show that the car has received its regular bodywork inspection. Those cars that have slipped out of the official network may not be at a disadvantage here, particularly if they have been looked after by a well-known independent specialist. Nonetheless, it is recommended that you give every car a thorough checkover, looking at least for small rust scabs and stone chips that have gone bad.

Pre-2000 models were fitted with door catches that bolted direct to the body and rust could develop under these after the catch bolts were overtightened on the production line. The fix (on 2000 and later models) was to fit a plastic gasket between the two metal parts. This can be done on earlier cars, if they have not already been retrofitted.

If you find more serious corrosion during your inspection, then be very suspicious – it could be evidence of poorly repaired accident damage, so investigate further.

Look along panels to see if they're straight, and check panel gaps for consistency (they should be even). The doors should close with the same action and the front and rear compartment lids close without undue effort. And look under the car, inside the luggage compartment and under the carpets for signs of distorted metal and repairs.

The deformable front and

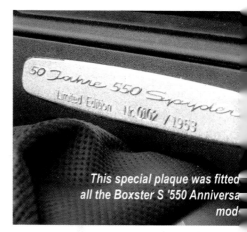

The paint code label is on the left side of the front compartment

This special plaque was fitted all the Boxster S '550 Anniversa mod

Colour choice is important for desirability and market value. Speed Yellow is striking for photographs, but not always so popular in a marketplace that often prefers more conservative colours

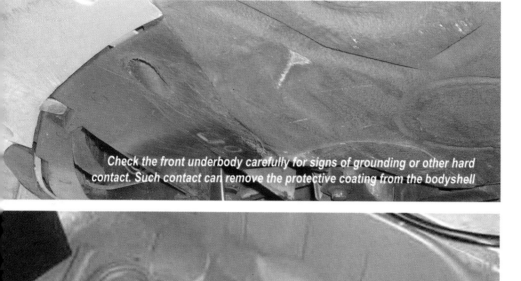

Check the front underbody carefully for signs of grounding or other hard contact. Such contact can remove the protective coating from the bodyshell

The inside of the front compartment with the carpet removed. Note the stove-in frontal area, indicating accident damage

rear bumpers are designed to withstand low-speed impacts without damage, so any substantial cracks suggest that the car has been in a relatively serious collision and you should investigate further. Small, hairline cracks in these panels, though, are not unusual.

Check below the front bumper and see if the front undertray has been damaged. This is low to the ground and so is particularly vulnerable. Look inside all the wheelarches

and examine the plastic liners for damage and any signs of careless paint overspray.

When you examine the cabriolet roof, check it closely from inside and out, looking for tears in the fabric and any other damage. Pay particular attention to the flexible plastic rear window in pre-2003 cars. Unless the window has been well-maintained with a special cleaner, it will have become scratched and/or brittle. The roof should never be folded when the temperature is less than 10

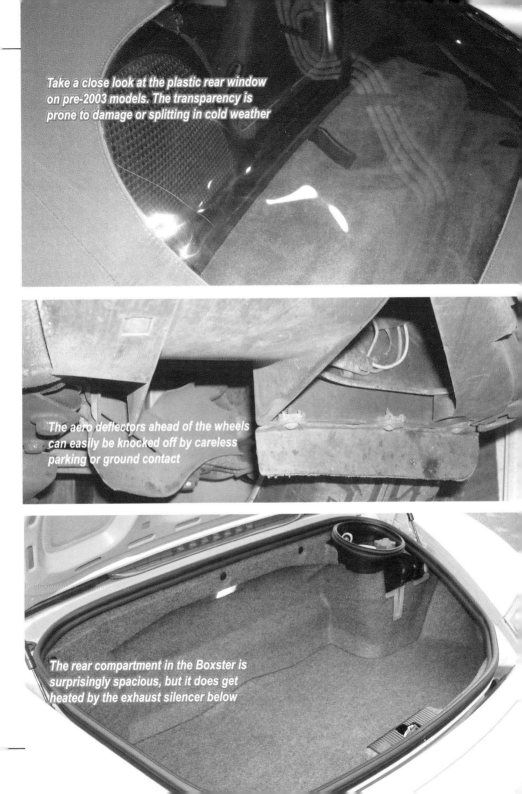

Take a close look at the plastic rear window on pre-2003 models. The transparency is prone to damage or splitting in cold weather

The aero deflectors ahead of the wheels can easily be knocked off by careless parking or ground contact

The rear compartment in the Boxster is surprisingly spacious, but it does get heated by the exhaust silencer below

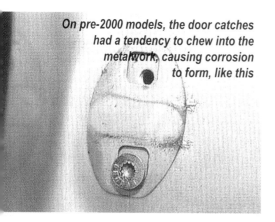

On pre-2000 models, the door catches had a tendency to chew into the metalwork, causing corrosion to form, like this

This early Boxster does not have climate control (air conditioning)

The climate control panel is simple to operate. Set the temperature on the left, fan and direction on the right

degree Celsius (50 Fahrenheit), as it kinks very easily, hardens when cold and can split. Ask the owner to fold the roof for you, don't do it yourself. If he or she stops half way through the opening cycle to smooth out kinks from the window, then it indicates a well-cared for car.

Although colour should not be your number one concern when buying a Boxster, it should be a consideration. You don't want your dream car to be a shade you don't like, and an unpopular colour can be hard to sell. Guards Red, Glacier White or Pastel Yellow aren't to everyone's taste! If you like these colours, then fine, but be aware that, everything else being equal, cars in these shades will be cheaper. On the other hand, the classic metallic silvers and dark blues are popular colours today and such cars are in more demand.

Equipment, trim and accessories

The value of a Boxster is strongly influenced by the number of options that it has fitted. Top of the list is full climate control (air conditioning), an almost essential fitment these days in any market. Any car without it will be discounted against one that has.

With the engine running and warmed, set the climate control system to automatic (by pressing the 'auto' button) and enter high and low temperatures to check the output is as required. There shouldn't be any other noises except the blower fans and if the output struggles to blow cold air, the air conditioning needs a service. The heating and ventilation system in general can suffer from failed switches and sensors, so it is important to check that everything works.

The Boxster comes with remote central locking and a factory fitted immobiliser. On early Boxsters (1997 and 1998) the alarm system was optional, but all later models should have this extra security.

Check that the electric windows and electrically operated exterior mirrors operate as they should. On pre-2000 cars, the windows automatically drop a few inches before the roof opens. On these early cars the windows have to be closed manually after opening or closing the roof.

What can ruin an otherwise good car is a badly installed after-market sound system, alarm or immobiliser. If the radio isn't a factory-fitted item (see the options list starting on page 42 of this guide), check the wiring under the dashboard and around the fuse panel (in the right-hand footwell). If it looks like a rat's nest of wires, leave the car alone. Poor electrical installations can totally upset the car's reliability.

Manually raise and lower the rear spoiler (using the switch in the outer side of the driver's footwell). It should operate smoothly and quietly with the ignition turned on.

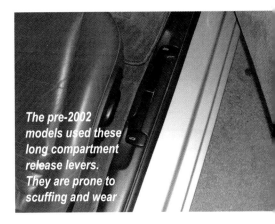

The pre-2002 models used these long compartment release levers. They are prone to scuffing and wear

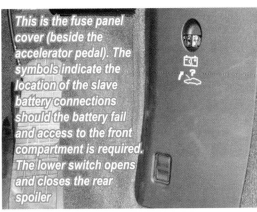

This is the fuse panel cover (beside the accelerator pedal). The symbols indicate the location of the slave battery connections should the battery fail and access to the front compartment is required. The lower switch opens and closes the rear spoiler

The simpler compartment release levers for the 2001 and later models

Full (ruffled) leather interior in Savanna works well wit
Lapis Blue external paintwork on this Boxster

*Porsche Communications Management
(PCM) is a desirable option that includes
sat-nav, cellphone and radio /CD*

Take care not to break any speed limits if you choose to check the automatic deployment of the spoiler at 75mph.

The large plastic headlamp covers on the Boxster may look attractive, but they are prone to scratching. Check the interiors of the covers do not suffer from condensation. Replacements for these light assemblies are relatively inexpensive, since many owners of the earlier cars choose to fit the lights with non-coloured turn indicator lenses. This means that the standard light assemblies (with amber turn indicator lenses) can be bought on the used market (try E-Bay and the specialist magazine classifieds).

Finally, when you start the engine, make sure that all the dash warning lights extinguish when you drive away. If they don't, investigate this further. In particular, if the ABS and airbag (if fitted) warning lights remain on, this can suggest that there is a potentially expensive fault with the systems (airbag warning light faults seem to be fairly common, but it can be the first indication the car has been involved in an accident).

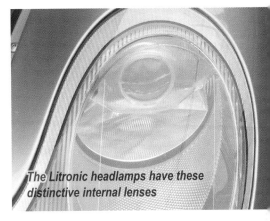

The Litronic headlamps have these distinctive internal lenses

Interior

The new generation, water-cooled Porsches made from 1996 are designed quite differently to the earlier cars, with a lot of emphasis on reduced assembly time. This means that most of the trim on the Boxster is attached by 'snap-fit' plastic clips or fasteners. These have a reputation for ageing or breaking and they do not like being taken apart and used again. If a car has several rattles or loose trim, it is a sure sign that the car has been apart for rectification in one form or another. These rattles will show themselves when you drive the car.

Simple door trim on a 1997 Boxster. Look for nicks in the material around the handle

The hinge of the stowage bin lid at the rear of the centre console is prone to breakage on pre-2000 models. The original is very flimsy and the new design is identified by the fabric strap limiting the lid's travel.

Wear and tear also often takes its toll on the bonnet and rear

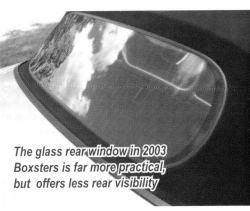

The glass rear window in 2003 Boxsters is far more practical, but offers less rear visibility

Full leather interior doesn't just mean the seat faces, but includes the dash, door trims and fronts of the roll-over hoops

The Boxster has Sports seats as standard, but check the faces and backs for damage. Note the odd scuff to the rear of this seat. Whatever had been placed behind the seats had damaged the door openings as well

compartment release levers. The pre-2000 cars had long, vulnerable levers and these can become very scuffed. Later cars had electronic releases using smaller, more robust switches.

Perhaps the most important desirability factor after air conditioning is whether a Boxster has a full leather interior. The Boxster (particularly the 2.5-litre models) has a rather austere plastic dashboard, door trims and centre console. Most cars were given leather-faced seats (and many a dealer claims a car has leather interior based on just this). But those cars with the full leather interior are the most sought after (because the leather trim extends to the dashboard, door trims, centre console and roll-over bar). The effect is to make the interior softer and more welcoming.

The interior is very durable, but does require a thorough check for damaged or loose trim. Look for driver's seats that have become worn and have tears in the material. Take out the overcarpets (if present) and check the main carpets for wear, particularly in the driver's footwell, under the heel of the clutch foot. The Boxster (unlike earlier 911s) has fitted carpets, so it isn't easy to remove them to look at the bodyshell underneath. Nonetheless, run a hand over the floor to check for any signs of dampness. If water is getting into the cabin, then either the door seals need attention or the roof is leaking.

Tatty carpets let the car down. However, this right heel mark demonstrates the value of overcarpets

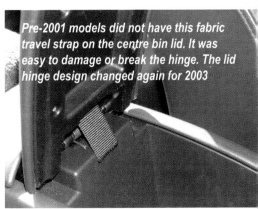

Pre-2001 models did not have this fabric travel strap on the centre bin lid. It was easy to damage or break the hinge. The lid hinge design changed again for 2003

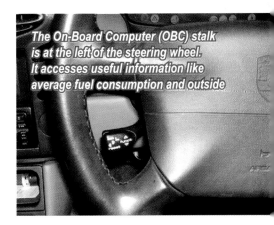

The On-Board Computer (OBC) stalk is at the left of the steering wheel. It accesses useful information like average fuel consumption and outside

On leatherette or fabric (Alcantara from the 2000 models), look for stains or rips in the material. All Boxsters will have some form of electrical adjustment on (at least) the driver's seat. Check the adjustment works in both directions. If seat heating is fitted, check that it works.

The door trims are robust, but the door handles have been known to break, but mainly it is wear and tear of the trim material around the handle that is the issue. The front and rear compartments have pre-formed carpets and these should be checked for splits and stains. It is advisable to remove the front compartment carpet trim to check the structure of the bodyshell for signs of accident damage.

Engine

The 2.5-litre water-cooled flat-6 was all-new in the Boxster. It has no relationship to the earlier air-cooled 911 engines at all (other than having the flat-6 layout). That said, the Boxster's engine is superbly engineered and generally major faults are rare.

The Boxster's water-cooled 6-cylinder engine, showing the clutch assembly

The first item to check is the engine oil. This should have been changed at the recommended service intervals (12,000 miles or the equivalent) or annually and these should be shown in the documentation. The oil should be high quality (Mobil 1 is typical).

The dipstick is accessed in the rear compartment. The oil cap should have no condensation and the oil on the stick should be brown rather than black. If there are any watery deposits visible (or if the oil appears pale or creamy), there could be a major problem with coolant entering

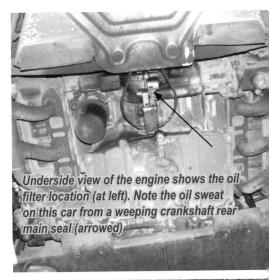

Underside view of the engine shows the oil filter location (at left). Note the oil sweat on this car from a weeping crankshaft rear main seal (arrowed)

Main item to check for on any Boxster is a leaking crankshaft rear main oil seal. A bad leak like this will be visible when you look under the car

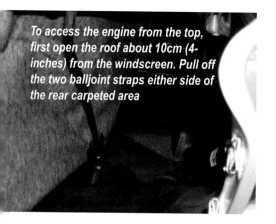

To access the engine from the top, first open the roof about 10cm (4-inches) from the windscreen. Pull off the two balljoint straps either side of the rear carpeted area

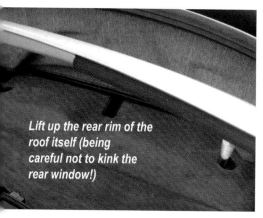

Lift up the rear rim of the roof itself (being careful not to kink the rear window!)

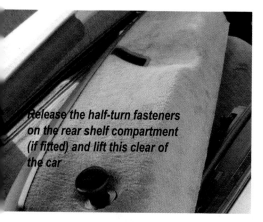

Release the half-turn fasteners on the rear shelf compartment (if fitted) and lift this clear of the car

the oil system. In this situation, don't buy the car.

The engine has hydraulic valve clearance adjusters and these can rattle for a moment when an engine is started. The adjusters work by filling with engine oil and if the engine isn't used for a while, the oil drains out. As long as the rattle disappears within a few seconds, then there is nothing to worry about.

It is important to look at the Boxster's engine from underneath. This requires the car to be raised safely, preferably on a professional lift and the removal of the plastic rear underbody. The underbody is retained by steel clips and 10mm bolts.

A number of Boxsters have shown a tendency to leak oil from the crankshaft's rear main seal (RMS). An oil residue will be apparent in the area around the rear of the crankcase and the gearbox. This problem appears to affect pre-2003 models. The resolution is to remove the gearbox and check the alignment of the seal to the crankshaft. If the alignment is good, then it is a simple matter to replace the seal. However, in a very small number of cases, the cradle supporting the crankshaft has been found to be out of alignment and replacing the oil seal in this situation will only give a temporary respite from an oil leak. In this situation, Porsche recommend engine replacement.

The Boxster can suffer oil leaks from corroded or broken supply pipes (including the one from the filler) and leaks from the lower camshaft covers.

When starting the car from cold (and especially after the car has been standing for some time) there may be a puff of smoke from where oil has pooled in the cylinders. As long as this doesn't persist, there shouldn't be a problem. Nevertheless, let the engine warm properly, be wary of an idle oil pressure less than 2 bar and listen for any unwanted rattles or resonances.

You will hear horror stories (particularly on internet foums) about other failures with both Boxster and the related 996 engines. Such failures are real, but they affect only a very small percentage of the overall water-cooled flat-6 engine population. For best peace of mind, we advise that you look for a car that has been serviced either by the official network or a recognised independent specialist. A Porsche warranty can improve that peace of mind still further.

It is important to repeat that if properly serviced, the Boxster engine has proven to be very reliable.

Transmission

The clutch on urban Boxsters can wear out fairly quickly. Some specialists have changed the clutch on cars with as little as 15,000 miles recorded. But this is rare and often there is a history of careless use.

Carefully used, a clutch should be

Release the half-turn fasteners holding the rear shelf carpet/sound proofing and lift this clear

Release the half-turn fasteners on the metal engine cover and lift this clear

Check the engine bay for leaks, frayed wiring or any signs of wear and tear. A dusty appearance is typical

The 5-speed manual gearbox from an early 2.5-litre Boxster

good for at least 50,000 miles. The tell-tale signs that the clutch is ready for replacement are juddering on driving away and slipping during acceleration. A slipping clutch will feel like the wheels are spinning, as if the car isn't actually in gear.

The gearbox is robust, but check

Tiptronic S shift comprises both a floor-mounted lever and steering wheel shift buttons

each gear for notchiness (worn synchromesh). Don't forget to try reverse.

The Tiptronic transmission is a popular option in urban markets, and there is little evidence that these cars have experienced any particular problems. The performance is slightly less than the manual, but this often isn't so important to drivers who want two pedal driving. Tiptronic is undoubtedly an industry leader when it comes to automatic transmissions.

As with any Tiptronic, check all its functions work as they should, both using the gear lever and the steering wheel buttons. Like the manual gearbox, the transmission casing should have no leaks at all.

If you like the automatic choice, then look for a post-1999 model. If the car is being driven in full automatic, the driver could select a gear using the steering wheel buttons. This instantaneous option lasts for eight seconds and is great for snap-overtaking.

Suspension and steering

The suspension is a conventional coil over shock absorber arrangement and is low maintenance. Check for leaks from the struts and look for damage to the suspension arms (normally accompanied by scrapes to the underbody). On older cars, lift the

The front suspension assembly uses rugged cast alloy lower control arms. Note here the good condition of the inner brake disc face

The rear suspension assembly shown with the gearbox removed from the car, with driveshaft at centre

This Boxster has a Tequipment (Porsche's own customisation brand) sports exhaust

Replacing the rear main seal on a Boxster means dropping the gearbox out of the car. RMS replacement takes a specialist about 4.5 hours

The water radiators are located in front of each front wheel

wheels off the ground and check for wear in the anti-roll bar bushes, steering rack and wheel bearings.

The wheel bearings are a wear item on the Boxster, both front and rear. Worn bearings reveal themselves on the move, with a constant whine or chuffing sound (but don't confuse this with normal tyre noise). Replacement is straightforward for a specialist.

When the car is elevated for engine inspection, check out the drive shaft rubber boots for splits and cracks. Good preventative maintenance of these can prevent a big driveshaft repair bill later.

Brakes, wheels and tyres

In normal use, the brake discs on a Boxster wear out from around 25,000 miles. Check the brake disc (and pad) wear by looking through the spokes of the alloy wheels. A torch will help for this. The wear limit for each surface of the disc is 1.5mm, assuming the disc is wearing evenly. If the disc has become grooved (particularly on the Boxster S, then earlier replacement is recommended. The grooves on cross-drilled discs are caused by pad material build-up in the drillings.

The face wear shows as a ridge at the extremity of the circumference of the disc. While the inner face is difficult to see with the car standing on the ground, if the outer face is worn, then assume the inner is worn also.

This Boxster has made heavy ground contact, breaking the underbody moulding and leaving deep scratches all over the underbody. With this kind of damage visible, check the suspension very carefully

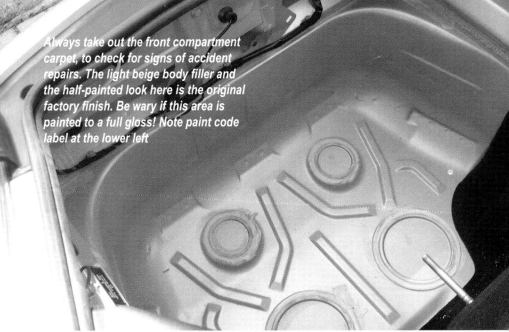

Always take out the front compartment carpet, to check for signs of accident repairs. The light beige body filler and the half-painted look here is the original factory finish. Be wary if this area is painted to a full gloss! Note paint code label at the lower left

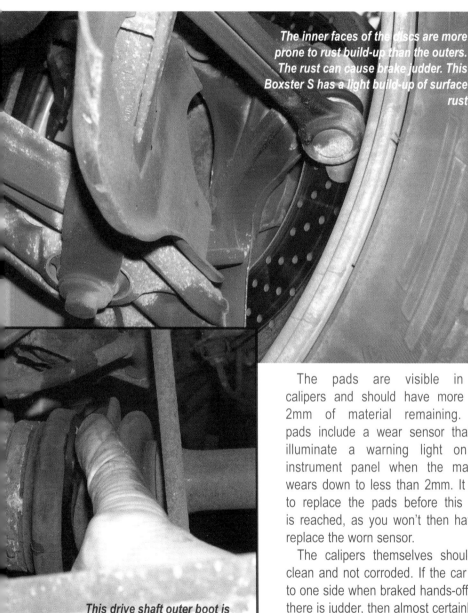

The inner faces of the discs are more prone to rust build-up than the outers. The rust can cause brake judder. This Boxster S has a light build-up of surface rust

This drive shaft outer boot is split and needs repalcement

The pads are visible in the calipers and should have more than 2mm of material remaining. The pads include a wear sensor that will illuminate a warning light on the instrument panel when the material wears down to less than 2mm. It pays to replace the pads before this point is reached, as you won't then have to replace the worn sensor.

The calipers themselves should be clean and not corroded. If the car pulls to one side when braked hands-off, or if there is judder, then almost certainly the problem is with the calipers or discs.

As you have probably already noted

there are a large number of options available for the wheels. The most important fit on an early Boxster are the 17-inch wheels. These improve the side view of the car significantly and should be considered a valuable addition. The 18-inch wheels increase that aggressive perception still further, but be warned the ride comfort is not as good (with the best ride being on the less fashionable 16-inch wheels).

Check the wheels thoroughly for corrosion and rim damage from kerbing or careless tyre fitting. Not only is it unsightly, but a badly kerbed wheel can be expensive to replace and it may have knocked the suspension out of alignment. Any balance weights should be glued (not clipped) to the insides of the rims, out of sight. Having the wheels refurbished is quite straightforward, but obviously the car will be off the road for about a week meanwhile.

Tyres should all be of the same brand and type, be worn evenly and they should be legal (in Europe, this means more than 1.6mm tread across three-quarters of the tread face). Tyres from a known, high-quality manufacturer suggest that a car has been well-looked after and that the owner has not skimped on costs.

And finally! Take out the toolkit and unroll it, look at the jack and the emergency tyre inflation compressor. Check everything is present, serviceable and correct.

This tyre has a chunk out of the sidewall from a hard kerb contact. It is not recoverable

Damage to the wheelrim from kerb contact

This heavily grooved drilled disc is ready for replacement

It is very easy to scrape 18-inch wheels, always check the wheel rims for this and for damage caused by careless tyre fitters

The tool roll may include the following items: 17/13mm open end spanner, 8/10mm open end spanner, right angle flat-blade screwdriver, 5mm Alley key brace, 17/19mm box spanner, 8mm box spanner, box spanner bar, Combi screwdriver with Phillips/flat blades,.

It is worth noting that toolkits have constantly evolved and the above list should only be used as a guideline.

Always check the condition of the discs and the pads. There should be at least 2mm of pad material remaining (any more wear and the sensor will also need replacement)

The emergency wheel houses the jack and toolkit

The Boxster's battery is at the rear of the front compartment

What to look for — at a glance

Engine rear main oil seal
Be sure to check for tell-tale spots of oil on the flo
where the car is normally parked. Look also for lea
from lower camshaft cover gaskets

Electrical
Ensure all the warning lights illuminate as the ignition is turned on and that they extinguish once the car has started. Check the windows, mirrors, wipers, indicators, lights, stereo and rear spoiler all work

Interior
Check bonnet and boot release levers on early cars as these are prone to damage. Check seat sides for scuffing and flip seats forward to check their backs for damage. Gear levers and door trims can be damaged by ring wearers

VIL sticker
Be sure to note all the numbers on the Vehicle Identification Label – applied under the bonnet and also in the service book. This gives details of the VIN, the colour code and the options (as codes, see page 32) fitted to the car at the factory

Tyres
Be sure to check the tre
depth (no less than 1.6mm in E
countries) across three-quarte
of the tyre tread. High pressur
and wheel misalignment can cau
uneven wear. Also ensure all tyr
are stamped with the approv
N-rating and are the same bra
and speed rating all round

Nose/bonnet
The front end is prone to stone chips. Check and if repainted, ask where the respray was performed (to ensure Porsche 10-year paint warranty is intact). Check under the front bumper for grounding damage and the headlamp lenses for cracking

Clutch rattle and judder
Check the clutch action when the engine isn't running. If it is noisy or heavy, it may need replacement. Any judder or slip when on the move confirms it

Leaks
Check the convertible roof for tears and wear, and that it operates satisfactorily. Check plastic windows for kinks and splits

VIN numbers
will find the Vehicle Identification Number sis number) stamped into a plate on the nger-side dashboard, just behind the creen. It is also found on a security label next driver's door catch. The number should agree ose on the VIL (see opposite) and in the car's ation document

Engine Oil
Check the oil level from inside with the electronic measure (under the speedometer). Also check the oil quality on the dip stick and oil filler cap. Foaming or creaming can suggest infrequent use, but may also indicate water in the oil and a potential engine problem

Body Panels
Look along the lines of the car to spot any small dents, imperfections, or 'orange peel' finish. Check the underbody, inside the wheel arches, compartment edges edges and all flexible seals for signs of overspray

Wheels/brakes
Carefully check alloy wheels for marks/chips and signs of poor refurbishment. Ensure they are original Porsche wheels and not after-market copies. Check brake discs for wear (corrosion and blocked holes)

About the author

Peter Morgan has a Bachelors degree in Mechanical Engineering and trained in the automotive industry. He has written for publication since his teens and became Technical Editor of Porsche Post (the magazine of the Porsche Club Great Britain) in 1981. He was Editor from 1991 to 1994. His first Porsche book, Porsche 911 -- Purchase and DIY Restoration was published in 1987. To date, he has written 12 titles on all aspects of Porsche, including racing, and his books have been translated into seven languages.

As a professional journalist, he is a member of the Guild of Motoring Writers and contributes to mainstream motoring magazines worldwide. He offers a personal, independent pre-purchase consultancy for Porsche drivers

Acknowledgements

To Porsche AG and Stephen Mummery for the use of various Boxster photographs used in this text. To Porsche Cars Great Britain and Porsche Cars North America for their help in supplying market-specific data. All other photographs are supplied by Peter Morgan Media Ltd.

Ultimate Buyers Guides include:

Porsche 911SC 1977 to 1983;
ISBN 0 9545579 0 5
Porsche 911 Carrera 3.2 1983 to 1989;
ISBN 0 9545579 1 3
Porsche 911 Carrera (964) 1989 to 1994;
ISBN 0 9545579 3 X
Porsche 911 Carrera (993) 1993 to 1998;
ISBN 0 9545579 2 1
Porsche Boxster & Boxster S 1996 to 2005;
ISBN 0 9549990 0 2
Porsche 911 Carrera, Turbo & GT (996)
ISBN 0 9545579 5 6
MGF and TF
ISBN 0 9545579 6 4
Land Rover Discovery
ISBN 0 9545579 7 2
Subaru Impreza (due Autumn 2005)
ISBN 0 9545579 8 0
Porsche 944 & 968 (due Autumn 2005)
ISBN 0 9545579 9 9

And watch out for new titles!